CONSERVING THE POLAR REGIONS

Barbara James

RSVP

RAINTREE
STECK-VAUGHN
P U B L I S H E R S
The Steck-Vaughn Company

Austin, Texas

Conserving Our World

Acid Rain
Conserving the Atmosphere
Conserving the Polar Regions
Conserving Rain Forests
Farming and the Environment
Protecting the Oceans
Protecting Wildlife
The Spread of Deserts
Waste and Recycling

© **Copyright 1991, text, Steck-Vaughn Co.**

Library of Congress Cataloging-in-Publication Data

James, Barbara, 1953-
    Conserving the polar regions / Barbara James.
      p.   cm. — (Conserving our world)
    Includes bibliographical references (p.46) and index.
    Summary: Focuses on the two polar regions, the Arctic and the
Antarctic, and dicusses their uniqueness, their relation to world
climate, their development and conservation, and the threat of
pollution.
    ISBN 0-8114-3458-3   Softcover Binding
    ISBN 0-8114-2393-X   Hardcover Library Binding
    1. Nature conservation—Polar regions—Juvenile literature. [1. Polar
regions. 2. Conservation of natural resources—Polar regions. 3.
Ecology.] I. Title. II. Series.
QH77.P64J35   1990   90-46064
333.78′216′0911—dc20   CIP
                                           AC

Cover: A dramatic sunset over the
Antarctic ice.

Series editor: Sue Hadden
Designer: Marilyn Clay

Typeset by Multifacit Graphics, Keyport, NJ
Printed in the United States.
Bound in the United States by Lake Book, Melrose Park, IL
    2   3   4   5   6   7   8   9   0   LB   95   94   93

Contents

The Last Wildernesses

The two polar regions, the Arctic and the Antarctic, are among the wildest, coldest, and most remote areas on Earth. There are long, dark, freezing winters when the sun never shines and short, cool summers when the sun shines 24 hours a day, giving the famous "midnight sun." In between are long days of twilight. In the winter, the frozen landscapes are swept by howling gales and blizzards that make life impossible for all but those specially adapted to living there. The summers can be dazzlingly beautiful with clear, blue skies. The sounds of the ice creaking and breaking are mingled with the calls of millions of birds.

Adelie penguins plunge into the sea off the Antarctic ice. These are one of the seven species of penguins that live in Antarctica.

The spectacular autumn colors of the Arctic tundra in Manitoba, Canada.

Few people live in the polar regions. In Antarctica there are no native mammals at all and no original peoples have ever lived on this continent. Only a small population of scientists temporarily live and work there in research stations. People have survived in the Arctic for thousands of years—the Inuit and the Lapps are well known for their unique lifestyles and cultures. More recently fishermen and workers in the oil and minerals industries have come there to work. The polar regions are two of the last wilderness areas left on Earth and have been relatively unchanged by human activity.

Poles apart

Where are the polar regions? Looking at a map of the world or a globe, the North Pole will be at the top and the South Pole at the bottom. They are the points farthest north and farthest south in the world and the regions that surround them are called the Arctic and the Antarctic. Seen from the air, the polar regions are huge areas bounded by the Arctic and Antarctic Circles. The circles are imaginary lines on the Earth, lying at the latitudes 66°32′ north and 66°32′ south; they circle all the land that has the midnight sun.

The Arctic

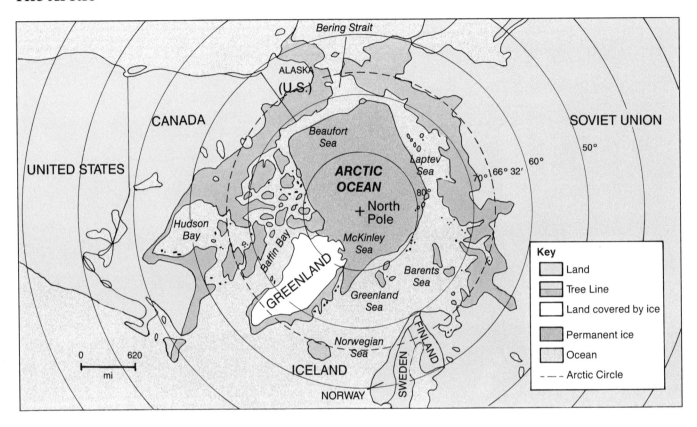

Key
- Land
- Tree Line
- Land covered by ice
- Permanent ice
- Ocean
- --- Arctic Circle

The center of the Arctic region is an ice cap, a vast area of permanently frozen ice floating on the Arctic Ocean. Around the ice cap is floating sea ice called pack ice. Farther into the ocean are hundreds of islands including Greenland, the world's largest island, which is also covered with a huge ice sheet. Bordering the Arctic Ocean are the northern stretches of the great continents of North America, Asia, and Europe.

The ice-free land in the Arctic has a tundra landscape. Tundra means "barren land" in the Finnish language. This land looks bare but is not barren. Many plants and animals live there successfully; they have adapted to conditions that

The partly frozen sea in the Granville fjord on the northwest Greenland coastline. Farther out to sea float icebergs broken off from glaciers that eventually reached the sea.

most humans would find impossible. The land is low and flat with many lichens, bushes, and tiny dwarf trees and occasional outcrops of bare rock. There is a permanently frozen layer of soil and rock called the permafrost, which can be up to 4,600 ft. thick. Above it is a thin layer of soil which freezes in winter and melts each summer. Because of the permafrost underneath, the water cannot drain away and thousands of lakes and bogs are formed. Warm ocean currents keep the Arctic warmer than the Antarctic; the lowest temperature is -90° F recorded in Siberia.

The tundra is not barren, but a special habitat for many plants and animals. The dwarf willow and birch trees are growing in Mount McKinley National Park, Alaska.

The Antarctic

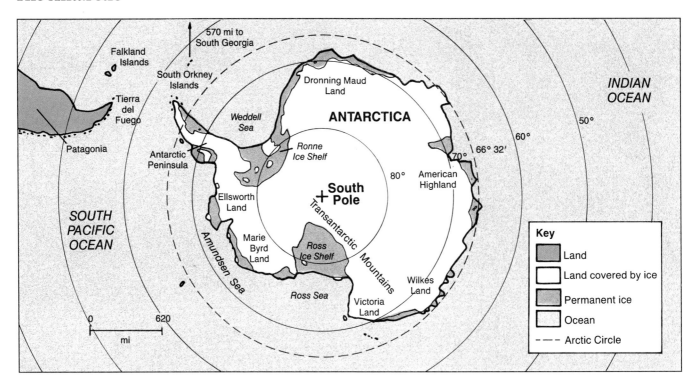

Whereas the Arctic is an area of ice surrounded by land, the Antarctic is its opposite. It is land surrounded by ocean, the southern waters of the South Pacific, South Atlantic, and the Indian Oceans. Antarctica is the fifth largest continent; it is twice the size of Europe. Its highest mountain stands at 16,857 ft. The land is covered by an ice sheet that has an average thickness of 1 mile.

Iceberg facts

Icebergs break off from glaciers that meet the sea. They vary greatly in shape and size. Nine-tenths of an iceberg lies hidden below the water surface. The photograph below shows Antarctic icebergs glowing at sunset.

The harsh Antarctic climate is never predictable. Two researchers from the British Antarctic Survey take samples of plant life during a summer snow storm on Signy Island.

Antarctica has 90 percent of all the ice on Earth and 70 percent of all the fresh water. Only a tiny area of the Antarctic coastline is permanently free from ice and here bare rock is exposed. On the oceans float huge blocks of ice called ice shelves. One, the Ross Ice Shelf, is the size of France. Ice breaks off the shelves to float away as huge, flat-topped icebergs.

The Antarctic is the coldest place on Earth where winter temperatures as low as -128° F have been recorded. Roaring, ferocious winds up to 100 mi. an hour produce blizzards and snow drifts, making the land almost impossible to live on. There is very little rain or snowfall. At the South Pole there is only about 2.75 in. of snow a year and Antarctica can be called a cold desert.

Why Are the Poles Cold?

The extremes of climate at both poles are caused by the angle at which the sun's rays hit the Earth's surface. They strike the Earth in straight lines but, because the Earth is curved, the sunlight which heats the Earth is spread over a wider area at the poles than the sunlight that hits the equator. The rays pass through more atmosphere at the poles, which means more of the sun's heat is absorbed before it reaches the land. The ice reflects some of the sun's heat back into space, making the areas cooler still.

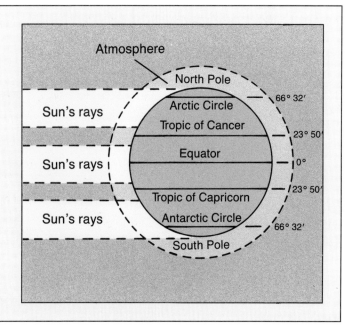

Differences Between the Arctic and the Antarctic

	Arctic	Antarctic
1	ocean surrounded by land	a continent of land surrounded by ocean
2	daylight months are March to September	daylight months are September to March
3	many ice-free areas	very little ice-free land
4	land, fresh water, and ocean habitats	mainly an ocean habitat
5	many animals and hundreds of plant species, including dwarf trees; land mammals such as polar bears and Arctic foxes	fewer animal and plant species; no land mammals
6	original human population, including Inuit and the Lapps	no natural human settlements; only temporary research bases
7	land and nearby sea is part of national territories	not owned by any country; under authority of the Antarctic Treaty
8	oil, gas, and minerals exploited; fishing; hydroelectric power production	fishing industry in oceans; mining exploration/exploitation banned
9	many military bases and growing military interest; can be used for weapons testing and storage of radioactive material	set aside for peaceful purposes; a demilitarized zone; nuclear weapons and storage of radioactive banned material
10	tourism well developed	little tourism but increasing

The pressures on the polar regions

The polar regions have always been difficult places for humans to live so, unlike warmer regions, there have been no major settlements or developments. However, with an increasing world demand for resources such as oil, fish, and minerals, developers are looking to the polar regions to exploit further sources. The polar regions are also under threat from pollution. Already they have been affected by air pollution from North America and Europe, toxic marine pollution, oil spills from tankers and pipelines, and from waste dumping.

What should we do with the polar regions? Should they be left as wilderness areas, shared by present and future generations of humans and other animals? Or should the vast polar resources of oil and minerals be used to provide energy and new materials for a growing world population? If they are, can industries develop in a way that is sensitive to the ecology of the regions, or will the Antarctic and Arctic be plundered with little respect for their unique landscape and wildlife? The future of the polar regions is of vital importance to our planet and concerns all of us.

Air pollution is posing an increasing threat to beautiful Arctic landscapes like this one on the edge of the Arctic tundra at 66°N in Kuusamo, northern Finland.

Unique Habitats

As wildlife habitats the two polar regions are very different. The more isolated Antarctic has fewer species of animals and plants than the Arctic and has no land mammals. Both regions have seals and whales but only the Antarctic has penguins and only the Arctic has polar bears.

The Antarctic habitat

In the Antarctic environment only two species of flowering plant can survive. However, there are over 400 species of lichens which grow on the few patches of bare rock, providing a habitat for several species of insect. With very few plants and no land animals, nearly all the Antarctic wildlife depends on the ocean for its existence.

The oceans are rich in food sources. In late spring and early summer, sunlight begins to reach the microscopic animals and plants (plankton) floating near the ocean surface. Through the process of photosynthesis the plants use the sun's energy to convert carbon dioxide, water, and minerals into carbohydrates, proteins, and fats. Water rich in minerals wells up from the ocean depths and acts as a fertilizer, increasing the production of plankton. These huge summer growths, or blooms, of plankton provide the basis of the Antarctic food chains. Plankton is the only source of food for krill, a tiny, shrimplike animal. Krill are less than 2 in. long but are the most important Antarctic animal. They are the food for millions of fish, birds, and sea mammals, such as seals and whales. The numbers of krill increase in summer, along with the plankton.

Colorful toadstools grow on moist moss in the milder climate of the South Orkney Islands. These islands lie along the Antarctic Peninsula.

An Antarctic krill. A record "swarm" of krill, seen in summer 1981, was estimated to be 10 mi. long and contain 2.5 tons of these shrimplike creatures.

The most numerous Antarctic mammal is the crabeater seal which, despite its name, feeds almost entirely on krill. There are estimated to be between five and eight million crabeaters, as well as five other species of seal: Weddell, elephant, Ross, fur, and leopard seals. Blue and humpback whales, which are also sea mammals, rely on krill for their food. These whales have special bristly baleen plates in their mouths designed to strain the krill from the water. Krills also form the principal food in the diet of millions of seabirds including the most famous Antarctic birds, the flightless penguins.

Right *An Emperor penguin chick huddles close to its parent. The chicks are raised in the brief Antarctic summer.*

Male elephant seals fighting for dominance on the Antarctic sea ice. These huge seals can reach 16 ft. in length and weigh up to 5,300 lbs.

The Arctic habitat

The harsh weather, ice cover, poor tundra soils, and short summers impose restrictions on plants and animals. Arctic plants can only grow slowly and are stunted in their development. A pine tree over 100 years old may be a dwarf with a trunk only 3 in. around. But there are over 500 species of wildflowers and when the Arctic summer does come, the tundra is a blaze of color. The flowering plants attract butterflies, wasps, and beetles, while the lakes and bogs provide the breeding ground for millions of mosquitos.

The short tundra summer attracts mammals. Caribou, or reindeer, migrate north through Canada to take advantage of the Arctic summer food supply. The huge herds of these deer are followed by wolves which prey off young or weak animals. Other Arctic mammals are voles, ground squirrels, lemmings, weasels, Arctic foxes and hares, musk oxen, and polar bears. In the sea there are seals, walrus, and whales. Birds also migrate to the Arctic in the summer to breed. Unlike the Antarctic, there are land birds as well as seabirds. Owls, swans, ducks, geese, and gulls are all found in the Arctic.

An Arctic bramble blooms on the Finnish tundra in June. The flowers provide pollen for insects. Later the berries are a source of food for birds and mammals.

The pale yellow Arctic poppy grows on bare, rocky ground in Greenland, Norway, and Sweden. It is adapted to survive the harsh climate.

Right *The colorful red-necked phalarope is a summer visitor to many Arctic countries.*

Below *A lynx chases a hare across the taiga, the northern forests around the Arctic Circle. The lynx is one of the few carnivores living in this region. It survives by feeding on smaller mammals, such as hares, weasels, and voles.*

Polar survival

Polar animals and plants have evolved several techniques for surviving in their harsh surroundings. Most bird species avoid the worst of the polar weather by leaving for warmer regions before winter arrives. Some travel thousands of miles on their migrations. The Arctic tern is the champion long-distance migrant. This bird flies between the two polar regions, spending summer in each of them. A few Arctic mammals, such as the caribou, move south in winter. But many animals, including polar bears, Arctic foxes, and some Antarctic penguins, spend the winter in the freezing conditions. Their thick fur or stored body fat enables them to survive. The frozen ground and lack of frost-free holes makes hibernation difficult, except for ground squirrels and polar bears.

Polar animals have even adapted their breeding cycles. They mate, give birth, and raise their young all within the short polar summer. By the time winter comes, the young must be ready to migrate or survive the polar winter.

Safety in numbers. Musk oxen form a defensive circle to protect themselves against predators, such as wolves. Their thick coats insulate them against the cold.

Right *The Arctic fritillary is one of the few butterflies found within the Arctic Circle. Here it is seen resting on a dwarf willow.*

Some wandering albatrosses breed on Antarctic islands, such as South Georgia. This chick is signaling to its parent that it is hungry.

Habitat destruction

Both the Antarctic and the Arctic have a wealth of wildlife. Some of the species are not found anywhere else in the world and others rely on these regions as a breeding ground. One of the major threats to polar regions is the destruction of habitats, the areas where plants and animals live. Mineral exploitation, tourism, and pollution all pose threats to these environments.

Arctic plant growth is very slow and land damaged by vehicles or human activity may take many years to recover. Without plant cover, the permafrost is easily damaged. The short food chains mean that life in the polar regions depends on a few key species: krill and silverfish in the Antarctic and Arctic cod, amphipods (marine crustaceans), and lemmings in the Arctic. If the populations of these few animals are changed, the lives of many others are affected.

Left *Arctic foxes feed on rodents, including lemmings. If the tundra habitat is damaged, populations of such prey animals could dwindle, also affecting predators like the Arctic fox.*

Rare, delicate plants like the Calypso orchid grow on the fringes of the Arctic. They could easily be lost if their habitat is disturbed by human activity.

Two polar bears on the sea ice near Churchill, Canada. Here they may be killed only by local peoples who have traditionally hunted them.

Conserving Polar Bears

The polar bear is the largest carnivore living on the land. It lives in the Arctic, spending much of its time on the pack ice and feeding mainly on seals. In the 1960s numbers of this beautiful white bear were declining rapidly, as hunting increased and their habitats were destroyed by oil and mineral exploration and development.

Six nations sent scientists to a meeting in Alaska to discuss the plight of the bears. As a result, a group was formed in 1967 by the International Union for the Conservation of Nature (IUCN) to coordinate the research and management of polar bear populations. The countries involved agreed to take measures to protect the bears: Norway and the Soviet Union introduced a complete hunting ban. The U.S., Canada, Greenland, and Denmark only allowed the bears to be hunted by local peoples whose lives have depended on them for hundreds of years.

The IUCN group continued to meet and in 1973 introduced the Agreement on Conservation of Polar Bears. This international agreement, which was renewed in 1981, ensures the polar bears' future. It requires the nations: to protect the habitats and wildlife, of which the bears are a part; to protect feeding and sheltering areas, as well as migration routes; to conduct research on populations and exchange results. Thanks to this good example of international cooperation, polar bears are now one of the best-researched and best-conserved mammals in the world.

Living at the Poles

An Inuit man prepares his sledge and husky dogs for a trip across the Greenland ice. Besides using dog teams, many Inuit ride motorized vehicles to cross the icy terrain.

The polar regions are not solely the habitat of wild animals. People also live there. In the Antarctic there are only scientists, temporarily living in research stations. By contrast, there are many different communities throughout the Arctic. The Saami, Khanti, Nenets, and Chukchi live in the Eurasian Arctic. The Aleut, the Dene (a group of Indian tribes), and the largest group of original Arctic peoples, the Inuit, live in the North American Arctic.

Saving the Inuit culture

The Inuit people have lived for thousands of years mainly on the coastal regions of Alaska, Canada, and Greenland. They were known as Eskimos but they prefer to call themselves Inuit, which means "the people." Traditionally they hunt and trap fish and sea mammals for food and clothing. Their art, music, and religious beliefs also center on this way of life.

The Inuit culture was first influenced by other people in the fourteenth century, when the first European whaling ships arrived. The whaling industry was highly profitable and grew, so that by the nineteenth century hundreds of ships were leaving North American and European ports to sail north. The foreigners disrupted the Inuit way of life, introducing tobacco, alcohol, and guns, as well as new diseases such as influenza, to which the Inuit had no resistance. By the 1920s the Arctic whales were hunted almost to extinction and the industry wound down, but the Inuit had been affected by the contact with the whalers; English was spoken instead of their own language, missionaries introduced new religions, and the old legends were lost.

Today, the Inuit combine modern and traditional lifestyles. They have supermarkets, computers, television, airplanes, snow vehicles, health centers and schools, but they are restoring their culture again through art, games, music, crafts, hunting, and trapping.

The Seal Hunt Controversy

Seals have been traditionally hunted by Arctic peoples for food, oil, and clothing. Hunting was originally on a small scale but it became a commercial industry as killing methods became more efficient, transportation easier, and as profitable markets for seal skins developed in North America and Europe. More seals were killed and the soft, white fur of the harp and hooded seal pups was especially in demand. Conservation organizations campaigned against the killing of the seals and they received huge public support in North America and Europe. This resulted in a ban by the U.S. Government on all sea mammal products, while the European Economic community (EEC) banned all seal products. This led to the collapse of the world sealskin market and economic disaster for the Arctic hunters. There have been bitter arguments about the seal hunt due to these conflicts of interests.

Right *A Greenpeace campaigner saves a harp seal pup by spraying its white fur with dye. The harmless dye makes the fur useless to the fur hunters.*

Above *Inuit hunters have killed a walrus. Such sea mammals provide food and clothing for the Inuit.*

Hostile environments?

The early travelers from farther south were used to different climates and conditions and to them the polar regions were harsh and hostile places. Over centuries the Arctic peoples had perfected a lifestyle that enabled them not only to survive, but also to utilize without abusing their environment. The travelers ignored this way of life and instead tried to enforce their own traditions often with disastrous results.

Arctic peoples have adapted to their harsh climate. Although many Inuit live in modern houses, they still build igloos when they are away on long hunting trips. A traditional igloo provides a warm, safe shelter against the elements.

This is a description by an English admiral who visited the Arctic in 1846:

> Nothing short of persecution could have driven them to take up their abode in these extreme parts of the globe, amidst the ice and snow . . . theirs, it must be confessed, is a most cruel and wretched lot . . . .

> *—Sir John Barrow*

Survival for the travelers became a challenge against nature which could only be met by technology. Today many people from other latitudes still hold this view. In contrast, the original peoples love their polar world, with its beautiful, open landscape and rich seas.

Modern technology is a part of everyday life for original Arctic peoples. Here in northern Norway a Laplander rides his snowmobile past a ski plane.

An Arctic Indian describes his life:

> Being an Indian means being able to understand and live with this world in a very special way. It means living with the land, with the animals, with the birds and fish, as though they were your sisters and brothers. It means saying the land is an old friend and an old friend your father knew, your grandfather knew . . . your people have always known . . . .

> —*Richard Nerysoo, 1977*

Research

Both the Arctic and the Antarctic have scientific research bases belonging to different nations. The scientists conduct research into the polar environments to learn more about their ecology, geology (including mineral reserves), and the atmosphere.

In the Antarctic the bases mark a country's presence on the continent. This strengthens national claims to the area, which will be important if mineral extraction is allowed to go ahead there. The conversation group Greenpeace has its own research base in Antarctica so that it can gain information about activities there.

Pollution—an Increasing Threat

Although the poles are at the ends of the Earth and seem remote, they have not escaped from one of the major problems of the late twentieth century—pollution. This has affected the land, sea, and air of polar regions.

Air pollution

In the Arctic, the Inuit began to notice that the skies were changing color. The deep blue skies were becoming whiter. Pilots flying through the area also noticed that the atmosphere was changing. What the Inuit and the pilots had seen was "Arctic haze" and scientists found that layers of pollution in the air were causing the haze. Waste chemicals from the industrial heartlands of North America, Europe, and the Soviet Union were discharged from factories into the atmosphere and were carried by the winds to the Arctic. The haze covers millions of square miles of Arctic atmosphere.

This wood pulp mill in Siberia in the Soviet Union contributes to Arctic pollution. However, factories such as this are necessary to produce paper, a product used by millions of people.

An ice-blue river cuts through a glacier in Greenland. Even in remote Arctic areas such as this, there is increasing evidence of acid rain pollution during the spring thaw.

For centuries Laplanders have herded reindeer. Pollution from the Chernobyl nuclear explosion has resulted in high levels of radioactivity in the animals.

Waste gases from the developed countries are also responsible for acid rain in the polar regions. Sulfur dioxide and nitrogen oxides are produced when fossil fuels are burned to provide energy for cars, power stations, and factories. Vast amounts of these gases are released into the air. They can be blown for hundreds of miles before they reach the ground as acid rain or snow. In the Arctic, the problem is highlighted in the spring and summer when the tundra snow melts, releasing acid pollution built up in the winter snowfall. Some lakes have become so acid that fish and insects cannot survive.

Nineteen countries have agreed to cut sulfur dioxide emissions by 30 percent to reduce the pollution problems, but scientists say reductions of 80 percent are needed for the acid lakes to recover fully.

Radioactive pollution

Radioactive fallout enters the atmosphere from nuclear waste and sometimes from nuclear accidents. One such accident had a dramatic effect on the Arctic. On April 25, 1986, a reactor at the Chernobyl nuclear power station in the Soviet Union exploded, sending a radioactive cloud into the atmosphere. The cloud drifted across Europe and Scandinavia, and one year later Norwegian scientists discovered high radioactivity levels in Lapland reindeer. Reindeer live on the tundra and their staple diet is lichen, a plant that is very sensitive to air pollution. The lichen had absorbed radioactive material, Caesium 137, from the Chernobyl fallout. Meat from hundreds of thousands of reindeer was too radioactive to be eaten and had to be buried in trenches 10 ft deep. Over the next five years the reindeer will continue to be slaughtered because they will still be contaminated. This will damage the economy and culture of the Laplanders which are based on the reindeer.

Marine pollution

The oceans are the dumping ground for many types of human waste, including industrial chemicals such as bleaches for whitening paper, and pesticides. These wastes also reach the oceans by seeping into the groundwater, streams, and rivers that eventually flow into the sea. Here the chemicals enter the marine food chains and are eventually absorbed by people when they eat certain fish.

PCBs (polychlorinated biphenyls) are chemicals used in plastics and electrical equipment. They are very difficult to break down and are very poisonous. They can only be destroyed by burning at 2,000° F. PCBs are now threatening populations of ocean mammals, and scientists warn that seals, polar bears, walruses, and some whales could become extinct because of them. Tests show rising PCB levels in their fat deposits or blubber. PCBs have also been found in the breast milk of Inuit women. There are fears that the chemicals can cause infertility in mammals, which would result in the extinction of many species.

Oil spills have affected both polar regions. The *Exxon Valdez* oil disaster in Alaska in March 1989 received much media attention. Less publicity was given to a similar Antarctic disaster: in early 1989 the sinking of a supply ship caused an ecological disaster in Antarctica. The *Bahia Paraiso,* carrying diesel fuel and gasoline, sank in the Bismarck Strait. The resulting oil slick hit Litchfield Island, an area that was protected because of its unique wildlife. The slick oiled penguins and other seabirds and huge numbers of krill died. In the cold polar conditions oil breaks down 100 times slower than it does in warmer climates. It may take up to 100 years for the area to return to normal.

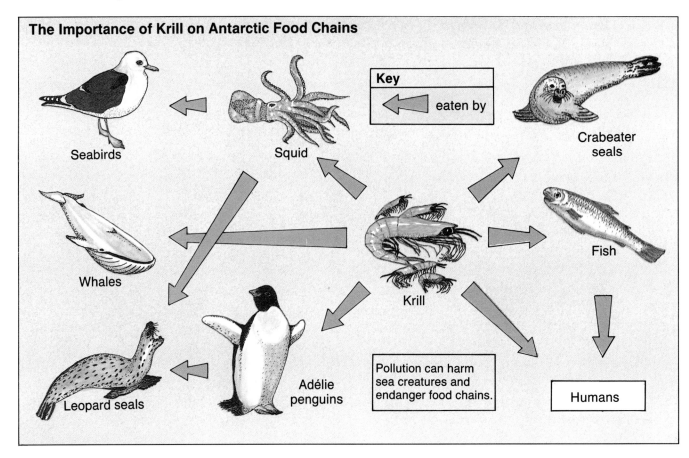

The Importance of Krill on Antarctic Food Chains

Key — eaten by

Seabirds · Squid · Crabeater seals · Fish · Whales · Krill · Leopard seals · Adélie penguins · Humans

Pollution can harm sea creatures and endanger food chains.

Antarctic research scientists continually monitor the environment for signs of pollution. Here New Zealand marine scientists sample seawater from 1000 ft. down in McMurdo Sound.

Garbage Dumps

Traditionally, the Arctic peoples had very little waste. Nothing was thrown away—food scraps and sewage were eaten by dogs and Arctic foxes. Today their lifestyle has changed and cans, plastic trash bags, packaging, abandoned machinery, paper, and sewage can all be found on frozen waste dumps throughout the Arctic. In the Antarctic Greenpeace surveyed research bases and found similar waste dumps causing an environmental hazard.

A garbage dump in Churchill, Canada. Such dumps are wasteful of valuable resources and a hazard to wildlife.

Polar Regions and the World Climate

Melting ice caps: the "greenhouse effect"

People worldwide are concerned about the "greenhouse effect." The Earth is surrounded by a blanket of gases called the atmosphere, which regulates the global temperature. The surface of the Earth is heated by the sun and the heat radiated back from the Earth warms the atmosphere before being lost into space. The atmosphere contains "greenhouse" gases such as carbon dioxide, nitrous oxides, methane, ozone, and the human-made chlorofluorocarbons (CFCs). These gases absorb the heat from the Earth more easily and therefore less heat escapes into space. The result is a warming of the global climate called the greenhouse effect. Just like glass in a greenhouse, the gases are trapped by the heat and kept under the dome they have formed.

Modern agricultural and industrial processes have increased the amount of greenhouse gases in the atmosphere. The extensive burning of rain forests, to provide farmland or make charcoal, releases vast amounts of carbon dioxide into the air. Over 5 billion tons of carbon dioxide and other gases are emitted into the atmosphere every year. Scientists are predicting that the world will warm up by between 2.7 and 8° F before the year 2030. This will cause the water in the oceans to expand and the polar ice caps to melt. Sea levels are forecast to rise by 5 ft in the next forty years, threatening the lives and homes of millions of people worldwide. Cities on the coasts, such as New York, Sydney, and Tokyo may be flooded.

Global warming is a threat to the unique icy landscapes of the polar regions.

How can we halt the greenhouse effect?

As people have become aware of this global crisis, they have looked for solutions. Reducing the amount of carbon dioxide emitted into the atmosphere is one answer. This means using less power and conserving energy, as well as developing alternative sources to fossil fuels. Wind, wave, and solar power are all renewable sources of energy that do not give off carbon dioxide, but so far there has been little government funding for research into their use.

There have also been efforts to reduce the amount of other greenhouse gases used, while CFC production and consumption have been cut.

The albedo effect

The ability of the Earth to reflect sunlight is called its albedo. This process helps maintain the balance of global temperatures. Light-colored regions of the globe, especially the snow- and ice-covered poles, reflect more of the sun's energy than dark-colored regions. The poles and other light-colored areas have a high albedo and dark-colored areas have a low albedo. If the polar ice caps become smaller because of the greenhouse effect, more land and sea will be exposed and less energy will be reflected back into space. This will decrease the Earth's albedo and add to the global temperature increase. The warmer climate may also melt the permafrost. If this happens, bacteria will rot vegetation in the waterlogged soils, producing methane, a gas which contributes to the greenhouse effect.

Alternative energy sources are one way of reducing carbon dioxide levels in the atmosphere. This hydroelectric dam at the source of the Nile provides electricity for Uganda. However, dams can cause other environmental problems, such as flooding of habitats.

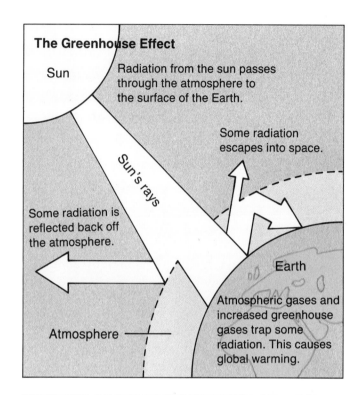

The Greenhouse Effect

Sun

Radiation from the sun passes through the atmosphere to the surface of the Earth.

Some radiation escapes into space.

Sun's rays

Some radiation is reflected back off the atmosphere.

Earth

Atmospheric gases and increased greenhouse gases trap some radiation. This causes global warming.

Atmosphere

The ozone hole

In addition to regulating global systems, the sensitivity of the polar habitats makes them good indicators of environmental change. Another environmental issue, the ozone hole, was first recognized in the Antarctic. In the mid-1980s, the British Antarctic Survey reported an alarming trend shown by ozone levels in the atmosphere over Antarctica. Ozone (O_3) is a form of oxygen that is produced and broken down in natural cycles. However, in the 1980s scientists observed that, each spring, the ozone level fell by about 40 percent, compared with the level in 1957. Later in the year the ozone level recovered.

Research centers such as the Eastern Arctic Research Laboratory in Canada monitor the climate and the atmosphere of polar regions.

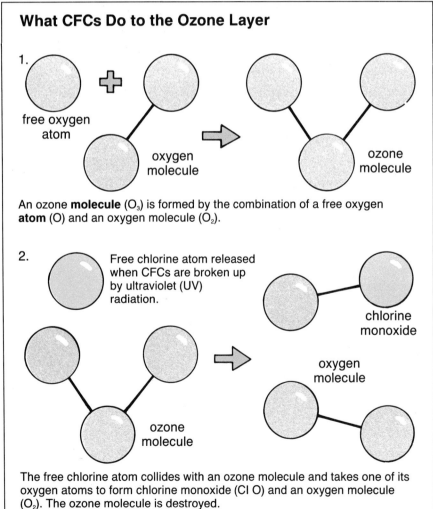

What CFCs Do to the Ozone Layer

1. free oxygen atom + oxygen molecule → ozone molecule

An ozone **molecule** (O_3) is formed by the combination of a free oxygen **atom** (O) and an oxygen molecule (O_2).

2. Free chlorine atom released when CFCs are broken up by ultraviolet (UV) radiation.

ozone molecule → chlorine monoxide + oxygen molecule

The free chlorine atom collides with an ozone molecule and takes one of its oxygen atoms to form chlorine monoxide (Cl O) and an oxygen molecule (O_2). The ozone molecule is destroyed.

Ozone is an important atmospheric gas. It is found in a layer 10-13 mi. above the Earth's surface and it shields the Earth from 99 percent of the sun's harmful ultraviolet (UV) rays. What the researchers had discovered was a hole in the ozone layer that allowed more UV radiation to reach the Earth's surface.

Life on Earth is delicately balanced and an increase in UV can upset that balance, causing serious damage. Ultraviolet rays can change the genetic structures of plants and animals and cause skin cancer in humans. In the Antarctic, increased UV levels prevent plankton from being able to photosynthesize, and this affects the marine food chains.

It has been the influence of human activity on a large scale that has caused the ozone hole. The chemicals CFCs are the main culprit. They are used in refrigerators, aerosol cans, and for cleaning electrical components. CFCs evaporate to become a gas and, along with other gases containing chlorine, nitrous oxides, fluorine, or bromine, they accelerate the rate at which the ozone layer is being broken down. Recently, scientists have begun to investigate the atmosphere over the Arctic. They have found ozone-destroying chemicals there too, but the damage is not so extensive yet.

The ozone hole and the greenhouse effect have been building up for decades and it will take decades for humans to improve the situation. A start was made in 1987, when 24 nations signed the Montreal Protocol, an agreement to cut the production of CFCs.

History in the Ice

The polar ice caps provide us with a unique record of the world's changing environment. Scientists drill into the polar ice sheets and remove a core of ice. The core sometimes contains particles of lead, radioactive fallout, dust from volcanic eruptions, and pesticides. These have circulated in the world's weather systems and have been laid down in the snow at the poles. As the layers of snow have crushed down, the particles have been preserved in an icy museum. The most recent deposits are near the surface of the ice.

The longest core so far extracted is 720 ft. long and at the bottom the ice is 160,000 years old. The core shows changes in the carbon dioxide levels in the air, and also records the ice ages and the polluting effects of the Industrial Revolution.

Scientists drill into the North Polar ice cap to extract ice for their research.

The richness of polar resources has attracted the attention of people interested in using them. The Arctic has been used for fishing, whaling, and the fur trade and, more recently, for oil and gas. The more remote Antarctic region remained relatively untouched until the whaling fleets arrived in the early 1900s, followed by large-scale fishing in the 1960s. In the future there is likely to be greater pressure on polar resources, as resources in other parts of the world are used up.

The world's last treasure chests?

The Arctic has vast reserves of minerals such as oil, natural gas, coal, copper, gold, and nickel and these are exploited by all the Arctic nations. Two-thirds of the Soviet Union's wealth lies within the Arctic Circle, including 65 percent of its oil, 82 percent of natural gas, and 73 percent of its mineral requirements. Enough coal exists in the Arctic to supply the world for 600 years. The North American Arctic has also been developed by the United States and Canada. Alaska now provides 20 percent of the total amount of oil and gas used in the United States.

Mineral extraction on this scale has changed the Arctic environment. There are huge drilling rigs, pipelines, tanker terminals, mines, and building complexes to support the people employed in the mineral industry. The industry brings wealth and employment to the areas but also brings pollution and the destruction of habitats and communities.

Inset *Miners preparing to dynamite the rock to extract iron ore from a mine at Kiruna, northern Sweden.*

The discovery of Alaskan oil has dramatically changed the local environment. Huge oil complexes tower above remote wilderness areas.

The Trans-Alaska Pipeline

Stretching 800 mi. across Alaska between the Prudhoe Bay oil field and Valdez on the Gulf of Alaska is the Trans-Alaska Pipeline. The pipeline, which took three years to build, crosses mountains, tundra, and forest in some of Alaska's wildest areas. Its construction shows how development and conservation can work together.

When the oil reserves were discovered and plans for a pipeline first suggested, conservation groups tried to stop the construction because of the damage it would cause to the Arctic habitat. They failed to stop the pipeline but did force developers to take into account environmental factors. The pipeline was moved to avoid important habitats and nesting sites of rare birds; work on the pipeline was halted during the peregrine falcons' breeding season; and the pipeline was raised in some places, so that large animals such as caribou could walk underneath it! The whole project was monitored by biologists with the aim that it would have the minimum impact on the environment.

Despite these safeguards some ecological damage did occur. Various habitats and migration routes were disturbed, vegetation was destroyed, and there have been oil leaks. A road built to run alongside the pipeline has opened up once-remote areas to tourists and poachers. But wildlife populations in the area are still healthy and the pipeline has not caused major environmental damage.

The Trans-Alaska Pipeline transports the oil to tankers, which ferry it to the U.S. and Europe.

In March 1989 Alaska suffered the worst oil spill ever in American waters. The tanker, *Exxon Valdez*, ran aground in Prince William Sound, one of the world's richest fishing grounds, spilling about 10 million gallons of crude oil. Shorelines were covered with oil and thousands of fish, birds, and sea mammals were killed. A huge public outcry prompted a clean-up operation but the scale of the damage was enormous. Since then, many Alaskans have reconsidered their view of the industry that earns them millions of dollars, and some projects have been postponed.

In the Antarctic, reserves of minerals and oil have been located by geologists but they have not been exploited because of the Antarctic Treaty, an international agreement signed in 1957 which bans any mineral development. However, in 1988, the Convention on the Regulation of Antarctic Mineral Resource Activities (CRAMRA) was set up, which allows the exploration and recovery of minerals as long as the environment is safeguarded. This agreement is highly controversial and conservationists, as well as some governments, fear for the future of this wilderness area if any mining begins. Others argue that mining in Antarctica is going to happen anyway so it is best to ensure that there are environmental guidelines.

After the 1989 Exxon Valdez *oil spill, a team of workers clean the oiled shoreline by hand in an operation that lasted several months.*

Right *Antarctic research bases are often maintained so that the countries that own them will have a claim to any future mineral exploitation. The photograph shows Soviet and East German bases.*

Alaskan brown bears and the salmon they eat are just two of the species that were affected by the Exxon Valdez *disaster.*

Harvesting the oceans

The polar regions also have large reserves of marine resources: fish, seals, whales, and krill. The Arctic is one of the world's richest fishing grounds, producing 10 percent of the world's fish catch. For the original Arctic peoples, the seas were traditionally their source of food and income, but today their fishing industry has been overshadowed by the huge long-distance fishing fleets from the Soviet Union, Japan, and EEC countries. These fleets have factory ships equipped with technology designed for large-scale fishing. Extensive overfishing has led to the depletion of some fish populations. North Sea herring stocks have declined from 4 million tons in the mid-1960s to less than 1 million tons today.

There is a similar story in the Antarctic. One of the finfish species was overfished by 1971 and a fishing ban was imposed to conserve the stocks. Even today, the populations have not recovered to their old numbers. As one fish species declined, the fishermen moved on to another species.

A trawler hauls in its catch of cod near the Lofoten Islands in northern Norway. Cod is an important food for many people in the world.

A harpooned minke whale is winched onto the deck of a Norwegian whaling ship. Most countries now, including Norway, have largely ceased whaling.

In the 1980s, the Antarctic fishing industry began to catch krill. Concern about the effect this might have on the marine ecosystem led to a huge international research program, and to the setting up of the Convention on the Conservation of Antarctic Marine Living Resources (CCAMLR) under the Antarctic Treaty. CCAMLR is a fishing agreement that protects the whole ecosystem.

Conservation measures include monitoring the wildlife and a catch-reporting system. Fishing bans can be imposed to protect any species in danger. At present about 40,000 tons of krill a year are caught mainly by the Soviet Union and Japan and, although this does not threaten krill stocks, the effects on krill-feeders, such as whales and seals, need to be monitored.

Tourism

Tourism is another area where conservation clashes with development. In the Arctic, tourism is a well-established industry and there are wildlife tours, and trekking and hunting trips. By visiting these beautiful, wild places, many people understand more about them and the need for conserving them. Tourism also brings income to the areas and local people. On the other hand, tourists can disturb the very habitats and wildlife they are coming to see; shy animals can be frightened by the tourists, whose waste and sewage can cause pollution problems. Tourism is becoming increasingly popular in the Antarctic, as more and more people wish to visit this unique and beautiful wilderness.

Below *Tourists and a polar bear come face to face in Arctic Canada.*

Settlements such as Jakobshavn in Greenland can provide a base for tourists to explore the region. The income from tourism benefits the local people.

In the Antarctic, the conservation debate centers around whether the area should be left as a wilderness area, where mining and other developments are banned, or whether its valuable resources should be exploited for the benefit of people.

In the Arctic, people are looking at how to continue to develop the region, while caring for the unique natural environment that exists there.

In the Weddell Sea, Antarctica, tourists photograph crabeater seals on an ice floe from the bow of the Linbald Explorer. *Increasing tourism in the Antarctic has to be carefully controlled if this fragile environment is to be preserved.*

A Safeguard for the Future?

Treaties and laws

The Arctic and the Antarctic have a different legal status. All the Arctic lands and adjoining seas come within the national boundaries and laws of the Arctic nations. They can use the land for whatever purposes they wish. The Soviet and American superpowers see the Arctic as an important area and they have military bases there, as well as weapons-testing and storage areas. There are some international research programs and agreements covering the Arctic, such as the Agreement on the Conservation of Polar Bears.

In the Antarctic all national claims have been suspended and the region is covered by the Antarctic Treaty. In the 1950s many nations had economic, scientific, and political interests in Antarctica but international cooperation over scientific research led to the signing of the Antarctic Treaty in 1959 by twelve governments. The treaty was unique because it stated that the continent was for ''free and non-political scientific research in the interest of all mankind.''

The treaty is the cornerstone of conservation policy in Antarctica. Two wildlife conventions have been negotiated, the International Convention for the Conservation of Antarctic Seals and the Convention for the Conservation of Antarctic Marine Living Resources. The Antarctic Treaty was enforced in 1961 with the understanding that after a period of thirty years, any one of the original nations who signed it may request a review meeting. This provision, along with the 1988 Convention on the Regulation of Antarctic Mineral Resource Activities, means that the future of Antarctica is uncertain.

A photograph taken at the South Pole, showing the flags of some of the nations that have signed the Antarctic Treaty since 1959.

At present, Antarctica is only populated by research scientists. Here an ice-breaker ship delivers supplies to the British Antarctic Survey base in the South Orkney Islands.

The World Conservation Strategy and global commons

The World Conservation Strategy (WCS) is a document published in 1980 by international environmental organizations. It outlines the environmental pressures being put on the Earth, and recommends ways of improving the situation. It calls on all nations to adopt conservation policies and for international cooperation to improve the environment.

The WCS especially draws attention to Antarctica as the only land mass on Earth that can be described as a "global common." A common is an area of land, sea, or atmosphere owned or used jointly by a community of people. The WCS recognizes how unique and vital Antarctica is and calls for "careful study and management of the living resources of Antarctica." In particular it urges the study of krill, as well as further research on the environmental impact of tourism, scientific research, and mining.

Hands off Antarctica! Early in 1989 Greenpeace campaigners protested against French plans to build an airstrip on this continent.

World Park Antarctica

In 1972 an international meeting organized by conservationists called on the governments of the world to make Antarctica a world park. This idea still stands but the world park cannot be established until it is supported by most of the countries in the world. Greenpeace has been campaigning for the world park and in 1987 set up the first nongovernment base in Antarctica.

The Greenpeace World Park base has a team of volunteers who carry out scientific experiments and weather observations. They also monitor the activities of other research bases, making sure that nations stick to the Antarctic Treaty.

The world park idea aims to protect Antarctica's wilderness and wildlife forever. Mineral exploitation, military activity, nuclear activity, and waste dumping would not be allowed.

The need for conservation

The polar regions are beautiful lands with wildlife not found anywhere else on Earth. We need to protect these unique wilderness areas, along with the wildlife and the original peoples who live in them. These regions regulate the global climate, and so the future of life on Earth may depend upon leaving these vast, icy areas untouched. Therefore it is in the interest of all humankind to ensure that these beautiful areas survive in the future.

Two moose bulls battle in Denali National Park, Alaska. National parks are important ways of conserving habitats, and the wildlife and peoples that depend on them; their preservation is essential for the benefit of future generations.

The Arctic

"Let the north of the planet—the Arctic—become a zone of peace ... What do we have in mind? First a nuclear-free zone in northern Europe ... peaceful cooperation in utilizing the resources of the Arctic ... coordinating scientific studies in the Arctic ... a unified complex plan for the protection of the environment of the north."

Mikhail Gorbachev, General Secretary of the Communist Party of the U.S.S.R., 1987

The Antarctic Treaty

The Antarctic Treaty was originally signed by the U.S., Argentina, Australia, Belgium, Chile, France, Japan, New Zealand, Norway, South Africa, Britain, and the Soviet Union. Other countries have since agreed to it.

It says: "it is the interest of all mankind that Antarctica shall continue forever to be used exclusively for peaceful purposes and shall not become the scene or object of international discord ... "

How you can help the polar regions

Although the poles are a long distance away from most people's homes and the problems there seem to be huge and overwhelming, individuals can take action in their daily lives which will positively help the Arctic and the Antarctic.

- Support conservation organizations that campaign to protect the polar regions and the wildlife in them.
- Learn about the environmental issues; tell people about the threats to these areas and write letters to newspapers, politicians, and anyone else you think ought to be more concerned.
- Avoid using products containing CFCs—look for "ozone friendly" aerosol cans.
- You can help to reduce the greenhouse effect: reduce your consumption of energy by switching off lights and heaters when they're not needed; wear an extra sweater rather than turn up the heat; have a shower instead of a bath; use public transportation to save fuel.

The Inuit culture has survived for centuries. If we care for our planet, the future of the Inuit will be assured.

Glossary

Adaptation The way in which an animal or plant develops in order to make it better suited to live in a particular environment.

Atmosphere The layer of gases that surrounds the Earth. Not counting water vapor, it consists of nitrogen (78 percent), oxygen (21 percent) and very tiny amounts of carbon dioxide, neon, argon, ozone, hydrogen, krypton, and pollutants.

Carbon dioxide A colorless, odorless gas found in the atmosphere; it is formed when fossil fuels are burned.

Carnivore An animal that eats other animals.

Convention An agreement made by a group of countries to work together toward a common goal.

Crustacean An animal that usually lives in water and has a hard shell, such as a crab.

Culture Group traditions that are passed on through the generations; includes religion, music, art, legends, and language.

Ecology The study of living things and the environment.

Ecosystem A community of plants and animals and the environment they live in.

Emissions Substances discharged into the air from factories, chimneys, and car exhausts.

Environment A plant's or animal's surroundings including air, water, and soil.

Extinction The irreversible point at which all members of a species have died out.

Food chain A chain of plants and animals through which energy is passed as they feed on each other.

Fossil fuels Fuels derived from organic (once-living) material like oil, coal, and natural gas.

Geology The study of rocks and minerals.

Glacier A river of ice.

Groundwater Underground water that comes mainly from water seeping down from the surface.

Habitat An area in which plants and animals live, such as a woodland.

Hibernation A process in which an animal's body functions slow down to allow it to survive very cold periods.

Ice shelf A huge thickness of ice attached to land but spreading out over the sea.

Infertility Not capable of producing young.

Latitude Imaginary lines around the world; lines of latitude are noted in degrees (°) north or south of the equator, which is at 0°.

Lichen A nonflowering plant.

Migration The regular, usually seasonal, movement of animals from one region or climate to another.

Ozone A form of oxygen that can damage plant growth and irritate the eyes and breathing system. However, ozone shields the Earth from the sun's ultraviolet rays.

Pack ice A large area of floating ice.

Photosynthesis The process by which plants use the sun's energy, water, and carbon dioxide to form carbohydrates. Oxygen is released in the process.

Plankton Microscopic plants and the tiny larvae of animals that live in the surface layers of the ocean.

Pollution The presence of harmful substances in the environment.

Radioactive fallout The fall of radioactive particles from the atmosphere to the Earth; they may come from nuclear explosion tests or a nuclear accident.

Resources The supplies of a material; often the source of economic wealth for a country.

Species A set of animals or plants that can be grouped together; animals or plants within a species can breed with each other.

Tundra A flat, treeless region with low shrubs, mosses, and lichens.

Wilderness An area uninhabited by humans.

Further Reading

Baines, J. *Conserving the Atmosphere* (Steck-Vaughn, 1990).

Finney, S. and Kindle, P. *Antarctic Explorations* (Good Apple, 1985).

Hargreaves, P. *Antarctic* (Silver Burdett, no date).

Hargreaves, P. *Arctic* (Silver Burdett, no date).

Hughes, J. *Arctic Lands* (Watts, 1987).

Lambert, D. *Polar Regions* (Silver Burdett, 1987).

Sandak, C. *Arctic and Antarctic* (Watts, 1987).

Seth, R. *Antarctica* (Chelsea House, 1988).

Soule, G. *Antarctica* (Watts, 1985).

Smith, J. H. *Eskimos-The Inuit of the Arctic* (Rourke, 1987).

Useful Addresses

Acid Rain Information Clearing House
Center for Environmental Information, Inc.
33 S. Washington Street
Rochester, NY 14608

Alaska Coalition
408 C. Street, N.E.
Washington, D.C. 20002

American Polar Society
c/o. Peter Anderson
125 South Oval Mall
Columbus, OH 43210

Friends of the Earth Foundation
530 Seventh Street, S.E.
Washington, D.C. 20003

Greenpeace U.S.A.
1611 Connecticut Ave., N.W.
Washington, D.C. 20009

Inuit Circumpolar Conference
Silarsuarmi Inuit Katuttiqatigiifingat
Post Boks 204
Godthaab 3900, Greenland

Sierra Club
730 Polk Street
San Francisco, Calif. 94109

Index

Picture Acknowledgments

The publishers would like to thank the following for allowing their photographs to be reproduced in this book: Bryan and Cherry Alexander cover, 6, 13 below, 14 right, 16 below, 19, 20, 21 above, 22, 23, 24 above, 25, 27 below, 30, 32, 33, 37, 38 left, 44; British Antarctic Survey 9, 12 left (R. Lewis-Smith), 40 (C.W.M. Swithinbank); Bruce Coleman Ltd. 5, 18 right (B. & C. Calhoun), 7 (Charlie Ott), 11 (Norbert Rosing), 12 right (Inigo Everson), 14 left (Pekka Helo), 15 above (Konrad Wothe), 16 above, 35 below (Eckart Pott), 39 (Jen and Des Bartlett). Geoscience Features 24; Greenpeace 21 below, 42. Oxford Scientific Films 13 above (Doug Allan), 17, 28, 35 (Ben Osborne), 27 above (Kim Westerskov), 31 (Stephen Mills), 36 (Doug Allan), 43 (Frank Huber). Rex Features 34 (J. Schultz). ZEFA 4, 8 (K. Graham), 15 below, 18 left, 29 (Slatter), 38 right (Sunak). The illustrations are by Marilyn Clay.